Oceans of the World

The Indian Ocean

By Lauren Gordon

Table of Contents

A Starfish Book
SEAHORSE PUBLISHING

Teaching Tips for Caregivers:

As a caregiver, you can help your child succeed in school by giving them a strong foundation in language and literacy skills and a desire to learn to read.

This book helps children grow by letting them practice reading skills.

Reading for pleasure and interest will help your child to develop reading skills and will give your child the opportunity to practice these skills in meaningful ways.

- Encourage your child to read on her own at home
- Encourage your child to practice reading aloud
- Encourage activities that require reading
- Establish a reading time
- Talk with your child
- Give your child writing materials

Teaching Tips for Teachers:

Research shows that one of the best ways for students to learn a new topic is to read about it.

Before Reading

- Read the "Words to Know" and discuss the meaning of each word.
- Read the back cover to see what the book is about.

During Reading

- When a student gets to a word that is unknown, ask them to look at the rest of the sentence to find clues to help with the meaning of the unknown word.
- Ask the student to write down any pages of the book that were confusing to them.

After Reading

- Discuss the main idea of the book.
- Ask students to give one detail that they learned in the book by showing a text dependent answer from the book.

The Indian Ocean

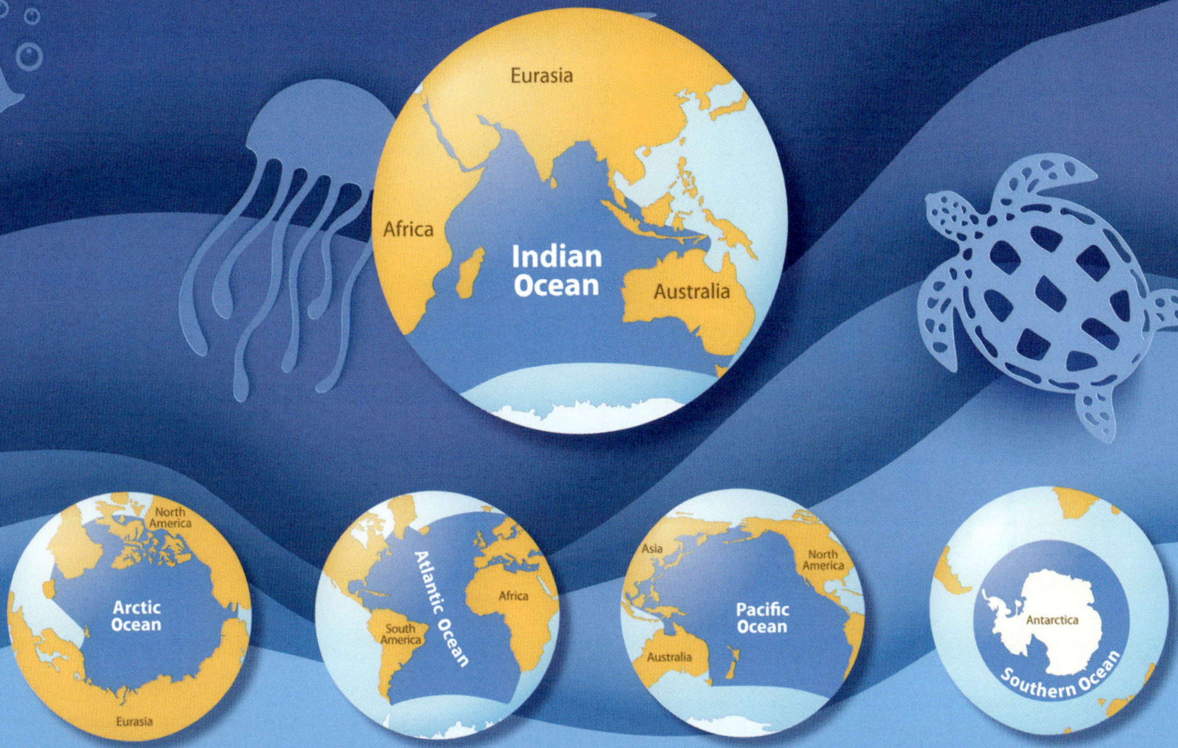

There are five oceans on Earth.
One is the Indian Ocean.

The Indian Ocean is found between southern Asia, Africa, and Australia.

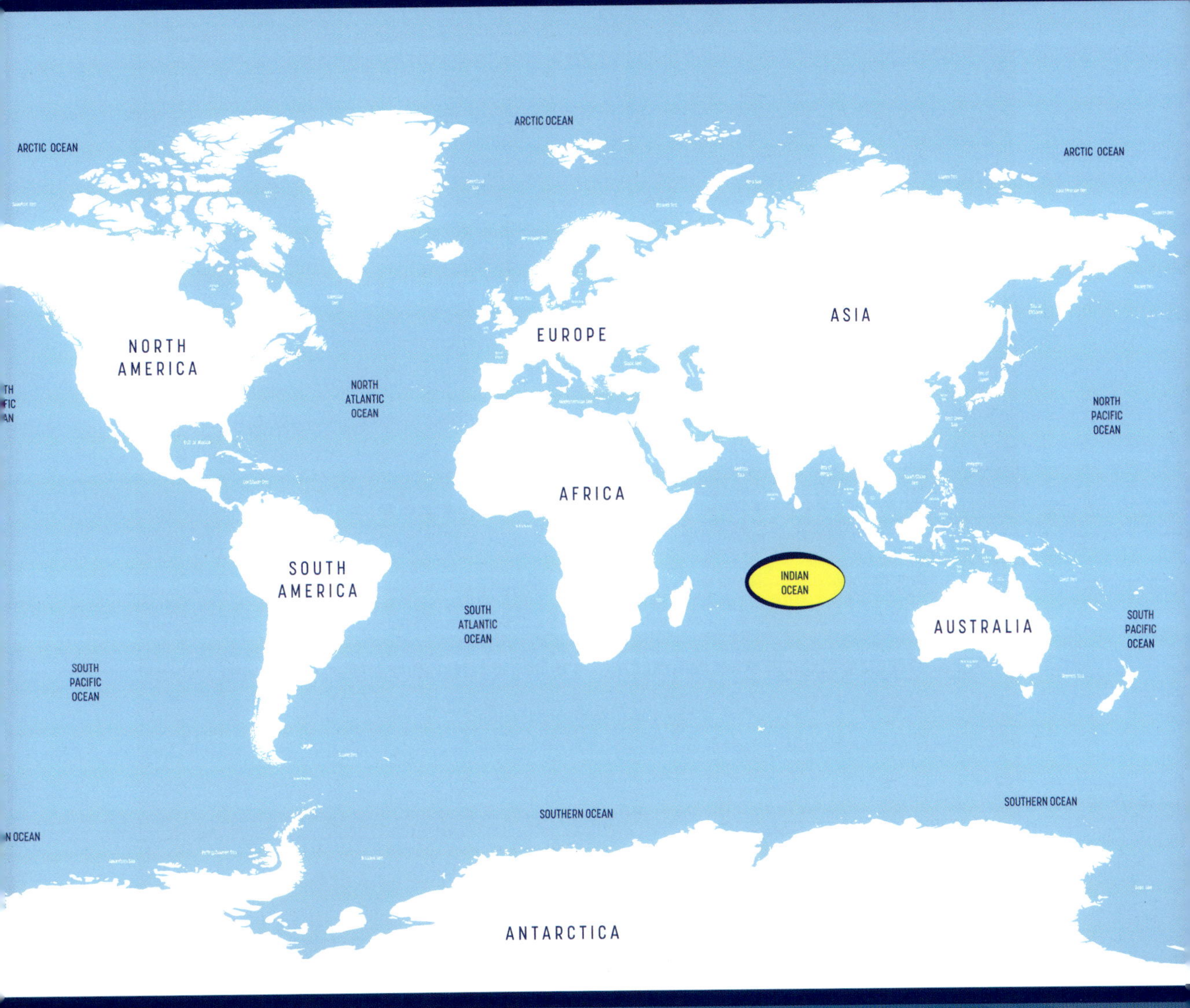
ARCTIC OCEAN
ARCTIC OCEAN
ARCTIC OCEAN
NORTH AMERICA
EUROPE
ASIA
NORTH ATLANTIC OCEAN
NORTH PACIFIC OCEAN
AFRICA
INDIAN OCEAN
SOUTH AMERICA
SOUTH ATLANTIC OCEAN
AUSTRALIA
SOUTH PACIFIC OCEAN
SOUTH PACIFIC OCEAN
SOUTHERN OCEAN
SOUTHERN OCEAN
ANTARCTICA

There are many **islands** in the Indian Ocean.

Some of them are Madagascar and Sri Lanka.

Hundreds of tiny islands make up the country of Maldives.

Lemurs live only in Madagascar.

The Indian Ocean got its name from the nearby country of India.

India **protrudes** into the Indian Ocean.

The Indian Ocean is the third biggest ocean in the world.

It is about the same size as five and a half United States of Americas put together!

United States
Indian Ocean

The Indian Ocean
is very deep.

It can be up to 23,000 feet
(7,000 meters) deep.

That is over five miles
(eight kilometers) deep!

The Indian Ocean is the warmest ocean in the world.

Warm waters make the Indian Ocean **vulnerable** to cyclones, tsunamis, and strong storms.

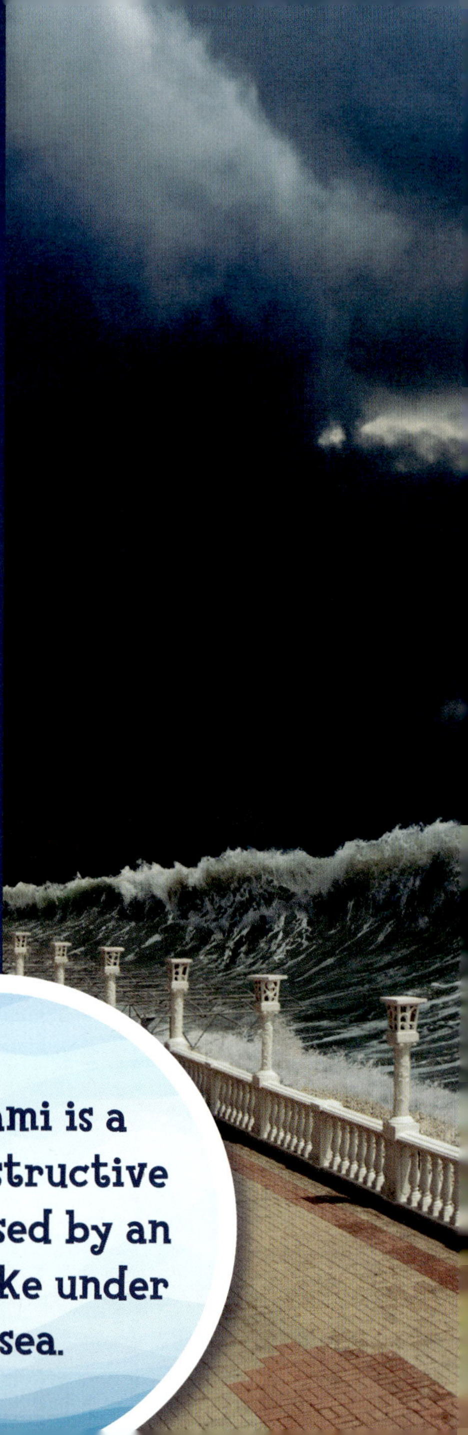

A tsunami is a giant, destructive wave caused by an earthquake under the sea.

The Indian Ocean's coral reefs are important **ecosystems**.

Laws protect coral reefs near Africa and Australia.

Thousands of species, or types, of fish and other ocean animals live in coral reefs.

Leatherback turtles live in the Indian Ocean.

Because of hunting and **pollution**, they are now **endangered**.

The leatherback turtle is the largest sea turtle and one of the biggest reptiles on Earth.

The Indian Ocean
is in danger.

It is changing as ice melts
at Earth's polar caps.

Earth's polar caps
are at the North
and South Poles.

North Pole
South Pole

Words to Know

ecosystems (EE-koh-sis-tuhms): communities of living things, including plants and animals, that share an environment

endangered (en-DAYN-jurd): threatened; in danger of becoming extinct

islands (EYE-luhnds): pieces of land completely surrounded by water

pollution (puh-LOO-shuhn): harmful materials that damage air, water, and soil, including gases, chemicals, and smoke

protrudes (proh-TROODZ): sticks out into

vulnerable (VUHL-nur-uh-buhl): weak and without protection

Index

Comprehension Questions

1. True or False: The Indian Ocean is one of three oceans in the world.

2. True or False: There are many islands in the Indian Ocean.

3. True or False: The Indian Ocean is the coldest ocean.

4. True or False: The Indian Ocean is home to the leatherback turtle.

5. True or False: The Indian Ocean is named after the country of India.

Answers
1. False 2. True 3. False 4. True 5. True

About the Author

Lauren Gordon is originally from New York and now lives in Florida. She lives with her husband and two children. In her free time, she likes to read and spend time with her family.

Written by: Lauren Gordon
Design by: Jen Bowers
Editor: Kim Thompson

Photographs from Shutterstock.com: Cover and p.17 image ©2015 V_E, backgound ©2012 Andrey_Kuzmin, water globe ©2012 zffoto; p.2 and throughout backgroud ©elic; p.3 and throughout background ©Aleksandra Bataeva, globes ©Designua; p.5 ©Pyty; p.7 ©2017 Hajakely, ©2014 javarman; p.8 ©2020 Dzerkach Viktar; p.9 ©2012 ixpert; p.11 ©2008 Alex Staroseltsev, ©2017 Harvepino; p.13 ©2021 Martin Prochazkacz; p.15 ©2013 IgorZh; p.19 ©2020 Giovanny Gava; p.21 ©2009 Intrepix

Library of Congress PCN Data
Oceans of the World / Gordon
The Indian Ocean
ISBN 978-1-63897-449-9 (hard cover)
ISBN 978-1-63897-564-9 (paperback)
ISBN 978-1-63897-679-0 (EPUB)
ISBN 978-1-63897-794-0 (eBook)
Library of Congress Control Number: 2021953369

Printed in the United States of America.

Seahorse Publishing Company
www.seahorsepub.com

Published in the United States
Seahorse Publishing
PO Box 771325
Coral Springs, FL 33077

SEAHORSE PUBLISHING